HOW TO Report on Books

We want to encourage our students to read more. We want to find out what they are reading. We want to find out what they are getting out of what they are reading. A time honored method for reaching these goals has been the book report. How we have them do this becomes the big question. *How to Report on Books* provides a wide variety of ways to approach the problem: Short and simple reading logs (which also require an evaluation of books read), an assortment of interesting paper and pencil reporting forms (kept short and simple for reluctant "reporters"), and book reporting activities involving oral presentations and art experiences.

Part 1 Activities with Books
pages 3-16

This section contains non-paper/pencil experiences requiring children to express their own creativity as they report on some aspect of their book.

Part 2 Book Report Forms
pages 17-46

Provides forms for a variety of written reports, some short and simple, others more detailed. They are designed to encourage students to read books in a variety of genre.

Part 3 Student Reading Records
pages 47-80

The 30 forms provided in this section encourage students to read more than one book on a topic. The books are listed on a reading log and then evaluated in a simple "check list" or "one-line" format.

Part 1

Activities with Books

Think about what draws you to try a new book. Did you read a review in the Sunday newspaper? Hear about it from a friend? Listen to the author being interviewed on PBS? Find yourself drawn to the colorful cover or interesting title of the book? All of these, and many other examples you may think of, can be adapted to book reporting techniques to be used by your students.

This section contains interesting ways to report orally or by creating a work of art. Each activity is described fully including materials to use, steps to follow, and ways to share the finished product. These activities may be assigned to individual children, partners, or to cooperative-learning groups. You may have the whole class work on one reporting technique or give your students the option to select the one in which they are the most interested.

Book Discussion Groups

Artist of the Week

Posters about Books

My Favorite Part

Cover It!

Sell that Book

Video Book Reviews

Puppet Time

Book Mobiles

Interview the "Author"

Book Dioramas

Who Am I?

Reading Discussion Groups

Book discussion groups offer an alternative to more formal book reporting. These book *sharing* groups bring two or more students together to discuss books they've read. Students motivate each other to read new titles they wouldn't have picked on their own.

The groups can consist of students:
1. having like-reading interests (mysteries, adventures, horse stories, etc.).
2. who have read different books by the same author.
3. who just love to read and want to share and hear about many different types of books.

Determine a minimum set of rules for these groups.
- Keep on the subject.
- Take turns talking.
- Be a good listener.
- Be tolerant of other opinions.

Set aside a time for the groups to meet once a week, once a month, whatever fits into your program and your students' interests.

When the groups are finished you may decide to have someone share briefly what was discussed.

Artist of the Week

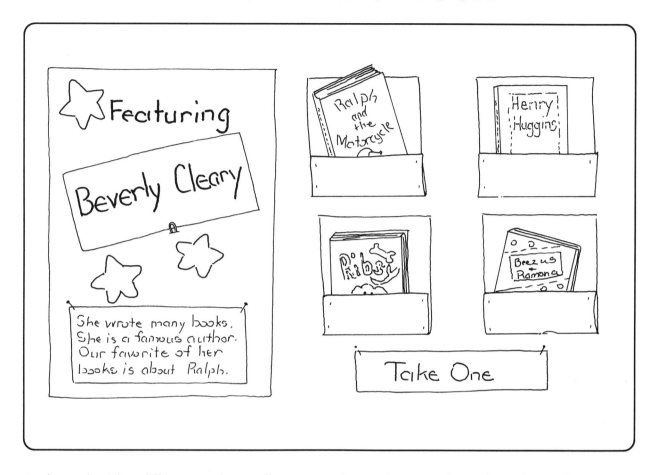

Each week pick a different author or illustrator to learn about. Find out about the author or illustrator's life, discuss the time in which they lived and list the books they created. Help students broaden their experience of different styles of writing and reading genres. Alternate nonfiction authors and picture book illustrators. Guide students into reading challenging fiction authors by beginning to read-aloud some of the text. Students are drawn to read books by authors they are familiar with, so use this technique to introduce them to authors and illustrators them haven't experienced before.

• Set up a corner in your classroom to display the work of the *Artist of the Week*. Have several copies of the authors or illustrators work to share with interested students. Keep a copy of an encyclopedia of writers and illustrators in this area so that students can look up information about the various artists.

• Use a portion of each day's schudule to read aloud to students from the work of the artist of the week. Children are never too old to be read to....so share examples of beautiful, interesting and informational books.

• Let students vote for their favorites. Keep a year long log of what has been read in class and the authors and illustrators that are "award-winners" in your class. Have an award ceremony and make blue ribbons for the books that are at the top of the list.

Posters about Books

Students make a poster to "advertise" the book they have read. These posters may be created from any medium in which your students are experienced. Display the finished posters around the room along with the book it advertises. Use this opportunity to get students into reading more and sharing what they read.

Steps to Follow:

If you have access to posters, bring some in for students to examine (try your local bookstore or favorite librarian to see if you can borrow some for a day).

1. Discuss with the group what needs to be included on a poster: book information (name of book, author, publisher, illustrator); "selling" copy (words/phrases to get someone excited about reading the book); illustration of major characters or event.

2. Have students make a plan on a small piece of scrap paper.

3. When students are satisfied with their rough sketch, they can make the poster.

Suggested Mediums:

1. Felt pen or crayon on large construction paper.

2. Tempera paint on large paint paper.

3. Torn paper on construction paper.

4. Watercolor and felt pen on white construction paper.

My Favorite Part

Discuss how each of these methods can be used by students to share their favorite part a book with classmates.

Students choose which way they wish to share their favorite parts. Provide time for them to prepare their presentations. One part of the presentation needs to be an explanation of why this is their favorite part. Another part will need to be a brief introduction explaining what has happened before in the story to prepare the audience.

1. **Read the Scene** - Students choosing this method need to practice reading the part aloud so they can present a smooth reading with proper emphasis and emotional overtones.

2. **Tell about It** - Students choosing this method need to think through the important elements of the scene. They need to plan what they will say. They need to practice the presentation until it sounds "right" to them.

3. **Act It Out** - Students selecting this method will need a bit more time. They need to decide how many people are needed to recreate the scene, whether props or costumes are necessary, and what words and actions are appropriate. The student/students presenting the scene need to practice until they feel they are ready to present it to the class.

 How to Report on Books

Cover It!

Have students make a new cover for an old book. This is a good way to expose students to "old classics" that lack the glossy, fancy covers but are rich sources of the written language. Offer to help your school librarian give the library a "face-lift" by developing colorful new covers for books that haven't been checked out in a while.

Before Beginning:

Each student needs to be aware of the information contained on a book cover. They should look at many newer volumes to see how the covers are organized. They need to know the title, the author and the illustrator. Are they also designing a spine for this book? Spines serve an important purpose in helping us locate books on a shelf. What goes on the inside fly-leaf? Will there be information about the author or a summary of the book? Does the name of the publisher appear anywhere on the cover?

Materials:

Felt pen on shelf paper is a dependable and easy-to-produce medium for creating the new covers. Use butcher paper if a volume is too big to be covered by shelf paper. All covers need to be laminated after the artwork is complete.

Steps to Follow:

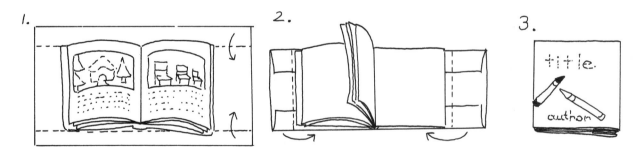

Sell that Book

Word-of-mouth is a powerful sales technique. By providing a "book selling" time for your students, you will be exposing them to new horizons of reading fun. Students will share with friends their feelings about the books they are reading. That commitment will force the reader to analyze as they read in order to have something to share with the group. It will also let the other students in the group glimpse books that they hadn't previously been motivated to try.

This process could take many different approaches. Students may do their selling before the whole class or in a smaller group. They may want to create audio-visual aids to use in their presentation. A poster, puppet or exhibit of items from the book may be useful. This process could be spontaneous as a part of a discussion group or it could be a scheduled report. The approach depends on the interest and response of the students.

What does a student need to know about a book to sell it?
- the author, illustrator
- the main idea of the plot
- the characters
- the setting
- the conclusion

This activity could be extended by providing the titles that have been reviewed in class availible for student check out. This is an automatic reward system for the *salesperson* who succeeds in getting another student to try his product.

Video Book Reviews

Make a video of a "book review" to show to the class. This is a group project. Students may review a single title or several books all from the same genre or by the same author. This technique requires a book reviewer to lead the interviews. This person could be a student, the teacher or school librarian. It is helpful if that person has read the books being reviewed.

Materials:
• the selected book or books
• video recorder (camcorder)
• props to be determined by the group
• music tape and tape player

Steps to Follow:
1. The interviewer and the person giving the review decide what questions will be asked and plan the answers. It may be possible to establish a set question format that students follow on all books. That would help students to think about the questions as they read the book.

> name of book
> author
> illustrator
> publisher
> short description of story
> strengths
> weaknesses
> final recommendation

2. The group finds a song or piece of music that is representative of the book being reviewed. The music is played at the beginning of the video and at the end.

3. The group determines the staging for the video session; two chairs, no chairs; outdoors, indoors; table, no table; etc. The person doing the video taping makes sure he/she knows how to work the video camera.

Puppet Time

Make cylindrical puppet characters to present characters from a favorite book. This simple technique can be used often to share good books with other students. These puppets are ideal because they are free standing and make a great display on book cases and counter tops in the classroom. Display them with the book they represent and watch those books move on to eager to readers.

Materials:

- large construction paper in several colors
- scrap box of paper
- scissors
- paste

- crayons or felt pens
- stapler
- junk box with buttons, pipe cleaners, feathers, etc.

Steps to Follow:

1. Student chooses a large sheet of construction paper to begin his character. He must either choose a color that represents his character or he will have to color it to match.

2. With the paper spread flat on the dest, details are added. Paper may be pasted on to create the details of this character or felt pen or crayon may be substituted.

3. Roll the construction paper into a cylinder. Lap it over in the back and staple the ends together.

4. Add any other details to create the desired effect.

Book Mobiles

Let students create hanger mobiles as a report on a favorite book. Encourage students to be creative with adaptations they might make to the basic design. These mobiles make an ideal addition to the room environment. They may be hung from the light fixtures or an improvised "clotheslines." This also makes a good free-time center activity to provide for students throughout the year. Save a table in the corner of the room for creating book mobiles with an assortment of interesting materials.

Materials:
- clothes hanger
- construction paper scraps
- string
- marking pens
- glue
- hole punch
- report form onpage 13

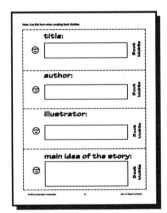

Steps to Follow:

1. Provide a chart listing information that needs to be provided with each mobile: author, title, illustrator, characters, etc. Cut rectangles from construction paper. Let students fill in the information with felt pen, punch a hole in one end and slip it over the hook of the hanger.

2. Students make the main characters from their story out of construction paper. They draw, color and cut them out. Holes are punched in the top of each character and a piece of string is tied through the hole. The other end of the string is tied to the cross-bar of the hanger.

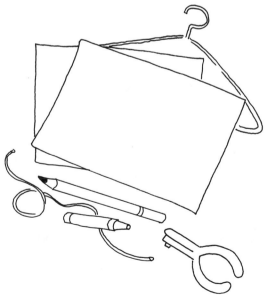

Note: Use this form when creating Book Mobiles.

title:

punch out

Book Mobile

author:

punch out

Book Mobile

illustrator:

punch out

Book Mobile

main idea of the story:

punch out

Book Mobile

Interview the "Author"

Simulate an interview by a talk show host with the author of the book. In the beginning, the teacher may act as the interviewer. The job of interviewer may pass on to an student as soon as the group understands the format. The student who is acting as the "author" must have read at least one book by that author. They must also be prepared with as many facts about that author as possible. A trip to the library to gather information about the author would add interest to this interview format.

Helpful Hints:

• The interview may be spontaneous and unstructured or it may follow a regular list of questions that would be provided ahead of time.

• The goal is to involve students in talking about books. The activity should be a positive and involving experience. Students should be encouraged to be a responsible audience when listening to the interview. Rules should be established as to correct responses and replies.

• This same procedure could be followed to create a mock interview of a favorite book character. What questions have you always wanted to ask Tom Sawyer or Winnie the Pooh?

Book Dioramas

Let students create dioramas showing an important scene from a favorite story. Students may do this as a group or they may create individual dioramas. These may also be made in a free-time centers that students use throughout the year. The finished products create an interesting room display; the may be put on cupboards, shelves, window sills, etc. Display the book with each of the dioramas.

Materials for Each Student:
• a box
• access to paper scraps of all kinds
• odds-and-ends such as:

sticks	rocks
paper tubes	fabric scraps
string	wire
clay	cotton balls

• paint and brushes
• scissors and glue

Steps to Follow:
1. Discuss what a diorama is and how one is put together. Explore the types of things that might be used to make the elements of the diorama. Talk about what parts of a book might be shared in diorama form (main characters, setting, major event from story).

2. Once children have decided what will go in their dioramas, provide ample time for construction to take place. You will need to have a place to keep incomplete dioramas while they are being put together.

3. Have students write the name of the book, its author, and a brief description of the story to be glued to the outside of the box.

Who Am I?

Involve students in the creation of favorite book characters from this easy-to-do and versatile paper folding and cutting technique. This technique allows students to create any character they wish using basic materials. The added value with this technique is that the character is created with a pocket in front so that notes, messages, or trinkets can be saved in it.

The finished characters can sit on a shelf or a desk. The front pocket might contain slips of paper with information about the book the character is from or trinkets that represent events in the story. These little cross-legged critters make a great contribution to classroom environment.

Materials:
- square sheets of construction paper for basic shape (any size will do)
- box of paper scraps for add-ons
- scissors
- paste
- stapler

Steps to Follow:
1. Make the basic shape with the square piece of construction paper.

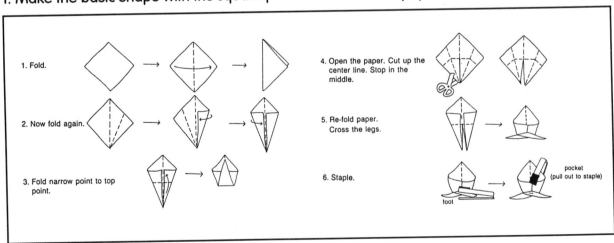

2. Add-on whatever shapes are necessary to create a particular story book character. This basic shape may be used to make people or animals. Encourage students to experiment to see what they can make work for them.

Part 2

Book Report Forms

These book report forms offer a variety of approaches to getting students involved in reading. The forms encourage students to read books in a variety of genre. The writing work required on these report forms is limited. We want students to spend more time reading and less time with a paper and pencil.

Students need to be familiar with basic book vocabulary and parts of books. They need to know where these items are found in a book, and to be able to identify these items in a story:

title	setting
author	plot
illustrator	copyright
characters	

These book reports were designed to move students into many areas of the library that they may not have sampled before. They will try books on: poetry, mystery books, how-to books, wild animal nonfiction, books about pets, sports, biographies, and fables.

Where will your students find books that suit their individual tastes? Which section in the library will they discover that they will go to again and again?

My First Book Report	*My Book Diary*	*An Illustrator Creates Pictures*
I like this book.	*Rate This Book*	*My Favorite Author*
Home Book Check Slips	*A Good Book Report*	*A Book Interview*
A Book Report	*A Book Riddle*	*My Favorites*
My Homework Book Report	*The Scariest Book*	*A Book Quiz*
A Garden of Good Books	*A New Cover*	*Report on a Book about Pets*
Book Worm Report	*Poetry Book Report*	*Reading about Sports*
The Bare Facts About this Book	*Survey of Popular Books*	*A Book Report on a Biography*
My Three Favorite Books	*Wild Animal Book Report*	*A Fable*
My Favorite Book Character	*"How To" Books*	*Books I've Read*

My First Book Report

My name is _____

The title of my book is

_____

_____

The author is

_____

_____

Do you like the story?

Do you like the
pictures?

Here is the best part.

Teacher: This page can be folded to resemble a little book.

Here is the best part of this story.

1 fold

2 fold

I like this book.

My Name

Title

Author

19

How to Report on Books

Home Book Check

_____ shared the book
Child's name

_____ by _____ with us.
Title · Author

Check

☐ _____ read the book to us.
Child's name

☐ We read this book to _____ .
Child's name

☐ We read the book together.

_____
Parent Signature

Homework—
Read a book!

Title: _____

_____

Author: _____

_____

Illustrator: _____

_____

Check

☐ _____ read this book to us.
Child's name

☐ We read this book together.

☐ We read the book to _____
Child's name

_____
Parent Signature

How to Report on Books

A Book Report

by_____

Title:_____

Author: _____

Illustrator:_____

The main characters:

_____   _____

_____   _____

_____   _____

The best part of the story:

_____

_____

_____

_____

_____

My Homework Book Report

by _____

I read a good book.

The title was [ ]

The author was [ ]

The illustrator was [ ]

How did the story make you feel?

☐ happy   ☐ sad   ☐ scared

Did you enjoy the pictures?

☐ Yes   ☐ No

Did you like the way the story ended?

☐ Yes   ☐ No

Would you tell your friend about this book?

☐ Yes   ☐ No

Why? _____

_____

_____

Make a picture of the best part of the story on the back of this page.

A Garden of Good Books!

Read a good book.
Fill in each part of the flower.

Setting

Main Characters

Title

Author

Why did you like it?

What happened in the story?

1. Cut out the flower.   2. Fold the petals.   3. Add a green stem and leaves.

Now add your flower to the flower garden board.

Book Worm Report

by _____

Title

Author

Illustrator

The Best Part:

How many pages?

Main Characters

1.
2.
3.

Was it a good book?

Yes   No   O.K.

The Bare Facts About this Book

by _____

Title
Name of the Book

Author
Who wrote it?

Illustrator
Who made the pictures?

Setting
Where did it happen?

Main Characters
Who was in the story? Tell the 3 most important characters.

1.
2.
3.

Did you like the story?   Yes

No

Give 2 reasons why:

How to Report on Books

My Three Favorite Books

by _____

You have____weeks to do this lesson.

Go to the library and read books.

Write your final choices here.

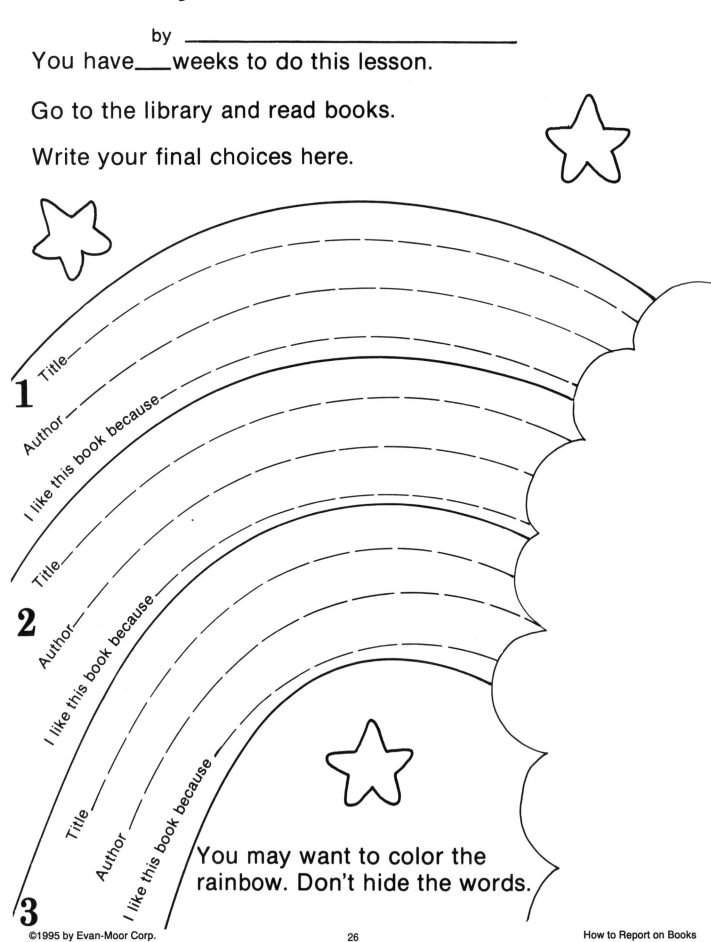

1 Title_____
Author_____
I like this book because_____

2 Title_____
Author_____
I like this book because_____

3 Title_____
Author_____
I like this book because_____

You may want to color the rainbow. Don't hide the words.

How to Report on Books

My Favorite Book Character

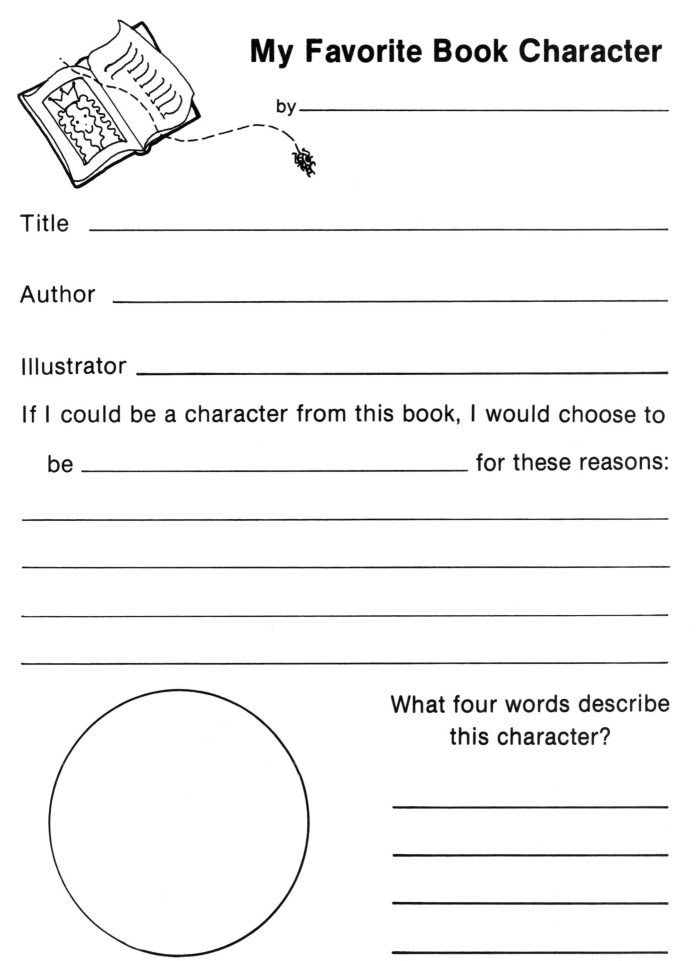

by _____

Title _____

Author _____

Illustrator _____

If I could be a character from this book, I would choose to

be _____ for these reasons:

_____

_____

_____

_____

What four words describe
this character?

_____

_____

_____

_____

This is what I would look like.

. How to Report on Books

My Book Diary

by_____

Today I began a new book.

The title is_____

The author is_____

Each time I read I discover something new.

My reading log:		About this book:
Date	Number of pages I read today	Characters—Who?
		Setting—Where?
		Main Idea—What?

I rate this book: good   fair   poor

Rate this Book

by _____

Title		©

Author		pages

Illustrator		setting

Color the bar graph to rate this book.

10 is good.   5   is O.K.   1   is terrible.

Characters	Plot	Ending	Overall Rating
10	10	10	10
9	9	9	9
8	8	8	8
7	7	7	7
6	6	6	6
5	5	5	5
4	4	4	4
3	3	3	3
2	2	2	2
1	1	1	1

Characters

Were they interesting?

Plot

Was it exciting?

Ending

Was it the best ending for the story?

Illustrate your favorite part of the story on the back of this page.

A Good Book Report

by _____

I just read a good book.

_____ told me about it.
(my friend's name)

It was entitled _____:

The author was _____:

The illustrator was _____:

It had _____ pages.

I liked the book for these reasons:

_____

_____

_____

_____

_____

I'm going to tell my friend _____ about this one!

A BOOK RIDDLE

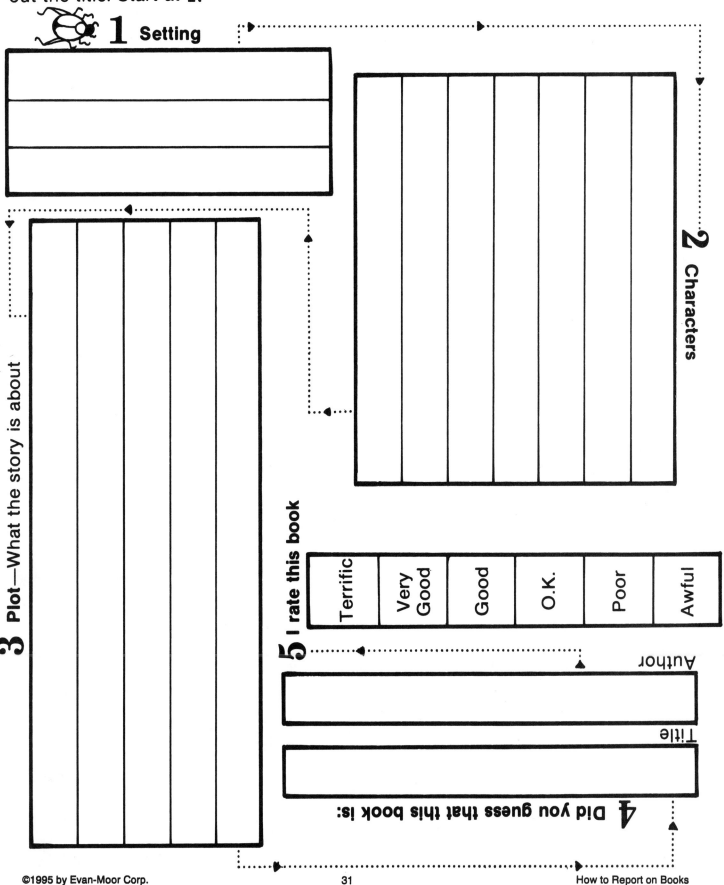

by _____

Can you guess which book I read? Follow the trail and see how soon you figure out the title. Start at **1**.

1 Setting

2 Characters

3 Plot—What the story is about

5 I rate this book

Terrific	Very Good	Good	O.K.	Poor	Awful

Author

Title

4 Did you guess that this book is:

The Scariest Book

Do you like to read books that scare you?   Yes

                                              No

I read one called _____

        written by _____

The main characters were   _____

                             _____

                             _____

The scariest part of the story was _____

_____

_____

_____

How scary was this book?   Score it for me.   Circle a number.

1	2	3	4	5	6	7	8	9	10

Not   A   Very   Super
scary   little   scary!   scary!!
                   scary

Would you give this book to a friend to read?

                                    Yes   No   Maybe

                                       How to Report on Books

A New Cover for an Old Book

Check List

☐ 1. Choose a book that has a worn or faded cover.

☐ 2. Read the book and decide:

Who are the main characters?	What is the main idea of the story?

_____   _____

_____   _____

_____   _____

☐ 3. Cut a sheet of shelf or butcher paper large enough to cover the book. Then:

   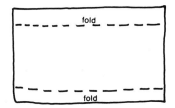   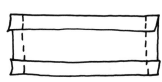

Fold top and bottom to the length of the book.

Fold in sides to fit book width.

See if it fits.

☐ 4. Remove the cover and put the title, author's name, and illustrator's name on the front.

☐ 5. Use the rest of the cover space to illustrate the main idea of the story.

    Be sure to:
        Cover the entire area.
        Make it bright and colorful.
        Outline the title in a dark color to make it clear.

☐ 6. Place the cover back on the book and show it to a friend.

Poetry Book Report

by _____

Which poetry book did you read?

title of this book

Were all the poems written by the same author?　　Yes　No

If yes, write the name here.

author of the poems

Did someone collect poems by different authors and put them together?

Yes　No

If yes, write the name here.

name of collector

Were there illustrations in the book?　　Yes　No

Get a sheet of paper. Copy your favorite poem from the book in your best handwriting. Illustrate the poem.

_____'s Survey of Popular Books

Put your name here.

★★

Ask 10 people to name their favorite book. Have each person tell you why it is a good book.

List each person and the book picked on this chart.

	NAME OF PERSON	NAME OF BOOK
1.		
2.		
3.		
4.		
5.		
6.		
7.		
8.		
9.		
10.		

Which one of these books would you like to read? _____

Why? _____

_____

_____

_____

     How to Report on Books

Wild Animal Book Report

by _____

Books about wild animals are interesting.

My book was about: (check your answer)

    O tiger   O bear   O otter

    O koala   O giraffe   O elephant

    O jaguar   O whale   O _____
                                                         another animal

Title [_____]

Author [_____]

Illustrator/Photographer [_____]

Is the book fiction or non-fiction? _____

List 3 facts you learned about this animal.

    1. _____

    2. _____

    3. _____

Draw a picture of this animal.

           How to Report on Books

"How To" Books

I found a book that showed *how to:*   **Circle your answer.**

make a mask	knit	fix a bike	fold paper
make puppets	sew	dance	train a dog
build an engine	paint	sing	cook

other _____

Its title was

The author was

The illustrator was

This book taught me how to _____

_____

_____

Now that I know how to _____, I'm going to try it myself.

Yes   No   Maybe

Did this book give good directions?

Directions
were poor.

Directions
were O.K.

Directions
were very good.

An Illustrator Creates Pictures

My favorite illustrator is _____

Illustrator's name

The illustrations can be found in these books:

Title

Title

Title

Title

_____ usually creates with:

Illustrator's name

pen and ink	watercolors	paint
pencil	torn paper collage	charcoal
colored pencils	block prints	other _____

I like _____ because:

Illustrator's name

1. _____

2. _____

3. _____

Now take a friend to the library. Share your favorite illustrations with your friend.

_____ is my **favorite author.**
Author's Name

I like books by this author because:

1. _____

_____

2. _____

_____

3. _____

_____

_____ has written these titles.
I have put a yellow line under my favorites.

_____

_____

_____

_____

(Use the back of this page if you need more space.)

Does this author write fiction or non-fiction?   _____

Does this author write books in a series?   Yes   No

Does this author also illustrate the books?   Yes   No   Sometimes

39   How to Report on Books

One student interviews another and fills in this form.

A Book Interview

Ask your friend these questions.

1. What was the title of this book? _____

2. Who was the author? _____

3. Have you read other books by this author?   Yes   No

   Name one _____

4. Who was the illustrator? _____

   Did you like the pictures?   Yes   No   O.K.

5. What is the setting of this book? _____

   _____

6. Tell about the characters in this book. _____

   _____

   _____

   Did the author tell you enough about the characters?   Yes   No

7. What was the plot of the story? _____

   _____

   _____

8. Was the story interesting enough to keep you reading?   Yes No Sometimes

9. Did the story have a good ending?   Yes   No

   Why? _____

                                                   How to Report on Books

My Favorites

by _____

If I were locked in a library overnight, I would choose my favorite books to help me pass the time. Here are some books I would choose.

Book Title	Why I would choose this book.
1. _____	_____
	_____
	_____
2. _____	_____
	_____
	_____
3. _____	_____
	_____
	_____
4. _____	_____
	_____
	_____
5. _____	_____
	_____

A Book Quiz

Ask yourself these questions.

Who is my favorite author? _____

Why? _____

_____

Which illustrator do I like best? _____

Why? _____

_____

These are the types of books I like best: (Circle the answers)

mysteries	adventure books	fables
science fiction	fairy tales	myths
animal stories	riddle & joke books	fantasy
sports books	books about history	biographies

others _____

I like to read fiction: Often   Sometimes   Never

I like to read non-fiction: Often   Sometimes   Never

I have read a book longer than 100 pages: Yes   No

My three favorite books so far are:

1. _____

2. _____

3. _____

_____'s Report on a Book
Your name
About Pets

Circle the pet from the book you read.

dog	guinea pig	turtle
cat	canary	fish
chicken	horse	_____
		other

Title _____

Author _____

Illustrator _____

List 3 things you learned about how to care for the pet.

1. _____

_____

2. _____

_____

3. _____

_____

Draw the pet.

Reading About Sports

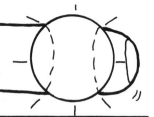

Check one answer:

___ Books about sports are my favorite.

___ I read sports books sometimes.

___ I've never read a sports book before.

Circle the sports you like to read about:

soccer	football
tennis	racquetball
gymnastics	racing
running	golf
hockey	swimming
baseball	_____
	(other)

List the best sport book you've read. _____

Why did you like it? _____

_____

Do you like to read about people in sports?   Yes   No

Who would you like to read about? _____

Why? _____

_____

Can you learn a sport by reading about it in a book?   Yes   No

Why? _____

A Book Report on a Biography

A **biography** is the story of an actual person's life. It tells what happened to that person and describes what that person did and felt.

I read the biography of _____

It was written by _____

List five facts you learned about the subject of the book.

1. _____

2. _____

3. _____

4. _____

5. _____

Is this person still alive?   **Yes   No**

Did this person live in the United States?   **Yes   No**

Why did someone write a biography about this person?

_____

_____

A Fable

A **fable** is a short story that teaches a lesson. The characters are usually animals.

I read _____
Title

by _____
Author

This book had   ☐ one fable

☐ several fables

My favorite fable in the book was _____

_____

The characters were _____

_____

The moral was _____

_____

_____

Do you want to read another fable?   **Yes No**

         How to Report on Books

Part 3

Student Reading Records

Encourage students to read in a variety of genres and keep a record of what they read. These reading record sheets can be used in many ways to strengthen student reading habits.

• Enrich thematic units by having students keep reading lists of all the books they read on the topic being studied.

• Use the forms in place of traditional book reports. Children are asked to record information about each book they read and make a short evaluation of its content.

• Encourage children to read from all the sections of the library.

• Motivate parents and children to read together at home on topics being studied at school.

• Use the forms as the basis for sharing about books in cooperative learning groups or for whole class book talks.

Space	*Eskimo Books*
Dogs	*Monsters*
Pumpkins	*Rabbits*
Bears	*Monkey*
Bats	*Animals Who Live in a Shell*
Humorous Books	*Whales*
Grandparents	*Native Americans*
Dinosaurs	*Snow*
Cats	*Alphabet Beooks*
Weather	*Hippos*
Rabbits	*Friends*
Biography	*Giants*
Elephants	

Books I've Read

Topic: Dogs

Title	Date	Author / Illustrator				Rating
		Author Illustrator	☐ picture	☐ fiction	☐ nonfiction	Rating
		Author Illustrator	☐ picture	☐ fiction	☐ nonfiction	Rating
		Author Illustrator	☐ picture	☐ fiction	☐ nonfiction	Rating
		Author Illustrator	☐ picture	☐ fiction	☐ nonfiction	Rating
		Author Illustrator	☐ picture	☐ fiction	☐ nonfiction	Rating
		Author Illustrator	☐ picture	☐ fiction	☐ nonfiction	Rating

How many famous dog characters can you name?

How to Report on Books

Topic: Pumpkins

Books I've Read

Date	Title		Rating
	Author	☐ picture	☆ OK ☹
	Illustrator	☐ fiction ☐ nonfiction	
Date	Title		Rating
	Author	☐ picture	☆ OK ☹
	Illustrator	☐ fiction ☐ nonfiction	
Date	Title		Rating
	Author	☐ picture	☆ OK ☹
	Illustrator	☐ fiction ☐ nonfiction	
Date	Title		Rating
	Author	☐ picture	☆ OK ☹
	Illustrator	☐ fiction ☐ nonfiction	
Date	Title		Rating
	Author	☐ picture	☆ OK ☹
	Illustrator	☐ fiction ☐ nonfiction	
Date	Title		Rating
	Author	☐ picture	☆ OK ☹
	Illustrator	☐ fiction ☐ nonfiction	

Put a yellow line through the one book you enjoyed the most.

Did you read any books longer than 50 pages?   yes   no

How long was the longest one?

How to Report on Books

Topic: Bears

Books I've Read

Can you name the largest bear?

Do you know how fast a bear can run?

Date	Title	Author		Name of bear in story:	☐ fiction
		Illustrator		Type of bear discussed:	☐ nonfiction
Date	Title	Author		Name of bear in story:	☐ fiction
		Illustrator		Type of bear discussed:	☐ nonfiction
Date	Title	Author		Name of bear in story:	☐ fiction
		Illustrator		Type of bear discussed:	☐ nonfiction
Date	Title	Author		Name of bear in story:	☐ fiction
		Illustrator		Type of bear discussed:	☐ nonfiction
Date	Title	Author		Name of bear in story:	☐ fiction
		Illustrator		Type of bear discussed:	☐ nonfiction
Date	Title	Author		Name of bear in story:	☐ fiction
		Illustrator		Type of bear discussed:	☐ nonfiction

Topic: Grandparents

Books I've Read

Date	Title	Author	Illustrator				Describe this grandparent:
				☐ picture	☐ fiction	☐ nonfiction	
				☐ picture	☐ fiction	☐ nonfiction	
				☐ picture	☐ fiction	☐ nonfiction	
				☐ picture	☐ fiction	☐ nonfiction	
				☐ picture	☐ fiction	☐ nonfiction	
				☐ picture	☐ fiction	☐ nonfiction	

Did any of the characters in these stories remind you of your grandparents?   yes   no

Topic: Dinosaurs

Books I've Read

Date	Title	Author Illustrator	☐ Fiction ☐ Nonfiction	Rating ☆ OK ☹
Date	Title	Author Illustrator	☐ Fiction ☐ Nonfiction	Rating ☆ OK ☹
Date	Title	Author Illustrator	☐ Fiction ☐ Nonfiction	Rating ☆ OK ☹
Date	Title	Author Illustrator	☐ Fiction ☐ Nonfiction	Rating ☆ OK ☹
Date	Title	Author Illustrator	☐ Fiction ☐ Nonfiction	Rating ☆ OK ☹
Date	Title	Author Illustrator	☐ Fiction ☐ Nonfiction	Rating ☆ OK ☹

Why do you think dinosaurs became extinct?

Topic: Cats

Books I've Read

Can you find fiction and nonfiction books about cats? yes

no

Date	Title	Author		Rating
		Illustrator	☐ picture ☐ fiction ☐ nonfiction	
Date	Title	Author		Rating
		Illustrator	☐ picture ☐ fiction ☐ nonfiction	
Date	Title	Author		Rating
		Illustrator	☐ picture ☐ fiction ☐ nonfiction	
Date	Title	Author		Rating
		Illustrator	☐ picture ☐ fiction ☐ nonfiction	
Date	Title	Author		Rating
		Illustrator	☐ picture ☐ fiction ☐ nonfiction	
Date	Title	Author		Rating
		Illustrator	☐ picture ☐ fiction ☐ nonfiction	

Do you have a favorite book on this list?
Put a red circle around the title of the
book you found the most interesting.

How to Report on Books

Topic: Biographies

Books I've Read

Biography A story of a person's life.

What is an autobiography?

Date	Title	Author	Why was a book written about this person?	When did this person live?

Did you find a biography that you would recommend to a friend? yes no

title

How to Report on Books

Topic: Alphabet

Books I've Read

ABCDEFGHIJKLMNOPQRSTUVWXYZ

Compare the alphabet books you find in the library.
Where did you find most of the alphabet books?

☐ picture
☐ fiction
☐ nonfiction

Date	Title	Author – Illustrator	What did **Z** stand for in each book?	Rating	Favorite Letters

Draw a yellow line under the alphabet book you enjoyed the most.

How to Report on Books

Topic: Whales

Books I've Read

Date	Title	Author	Was this a factual book? yes no	Did you learn something about whales? yes no
		Illustrator		Did you enjoy the book? yes ok no
Date	Title	Author	Was this a factual book? yes no	Did you learn something about whales? yes no
		Illustrator		Did you enjoy the book? yes ok no
Date	Title	Author	Was this a factual book? yes no	Did you learn something about whales? yes no
		Illustrator		Did you enjoy the book? yes ok no
Date	Title	Author	Was this a factual book? yes no	Did you learn something about whales? yes no
		Illustrator		Did you enjoy the book? yes ok no
Date	Title	Author	Was this a factual book? yes no	Did you learn something about whales? yes no
		Illustrator		Did you enjoy the book? yes ok no
Date	Title	Author	Was this a factual book? yes no	Did you learn something about whales? yes no
		Illustrator		Did you enjoy the book?

A whale fact I learned:

Topic: Native Americans

Books I've Read

Stories of Native Americans Today

Date	Rating: ☆ OK ☹	fiction ☐ nonfiction ☐
Title		
Author		

Date	Rating: ☆ OK ☹	fiction ☐ nonfiction ☐
Title		
Author		

Date	Rating: ☆ OK ☹	fiction ☐ nonfiction ☐
Title		
Author		

Native American Folktales

Date	Rating: ☆ OK ☹
Title	
Author	
Illustrator	

Date	Rating: ☆ OK ☹
Title	
Author	
Illustrator	

Date	Rating: ☆ OK ☹
Title	
Author	
Illustrator	

Nonfiction Books

Date	Rating: good information ☐ incomplete information ☐
Title	
Author	
Tribe	

Date	Rating: good information ☐ incomplete information ☐
Title	
Author	
Tribe	

Date	Rating: good information ☐ incomplete information ☐
Title	
Author	
Tribe	

How to Report on Books

Books I've Read

Topic: Bats

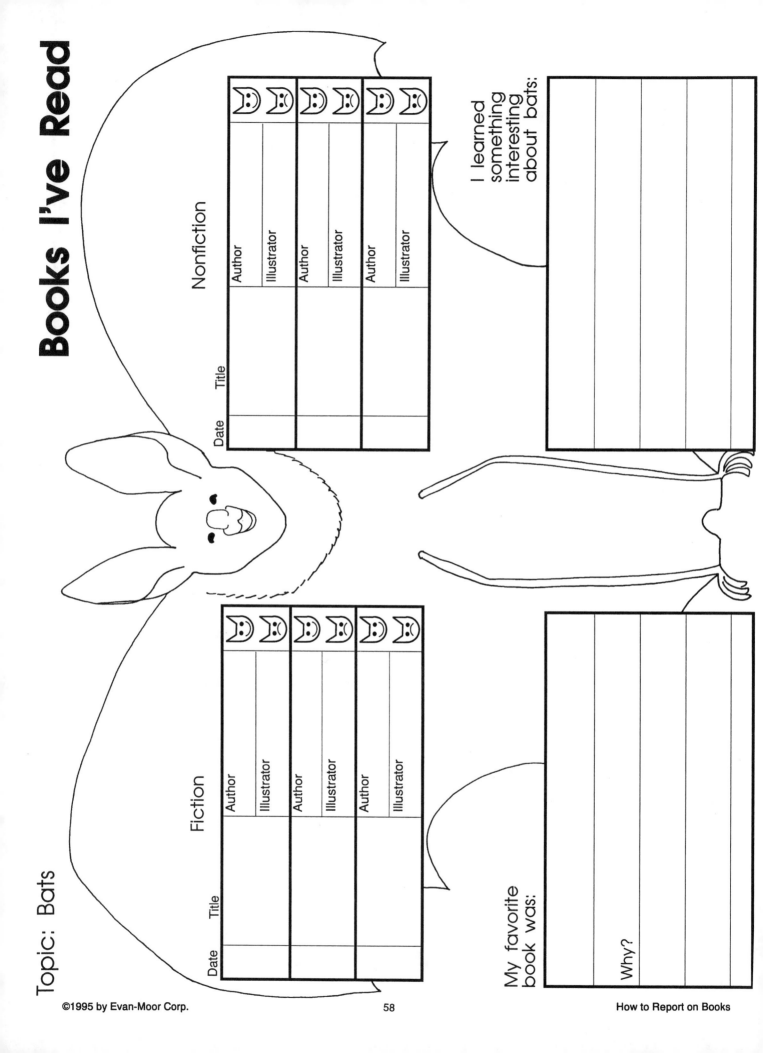

Nonfiction

Date	Title	Author		
		Illustrator		
		Author		
		Illustrator		
		Author		
		Illustrator		

I learned something interesting about bats:

Fiction

Date	Title	Author		
		Illustrator		
		Author		
		Illustrator		
		Author		
		Illustrator		

My favorite book was:

Why?

How to Report on Books

Books I've Read

Topic: Weather

Look for these conditions:

sleet, snow, rain, frost, thunder, drought, tornado, sunny, humidity, wind, evaporation, cloudy

Date	Title	Author / Illustrator		Pages	Rating
			□ picture □ fiction □ nonfiction		
			□ picture □ fiction □ nonfiction		
			□ picture □ fiction □ nonfiction		
			□ picture □ fiction □ nonfiction		
			□ picture □ fiction □ nonfiction		
			□ picture □ fiction □ nonfiction		

Have you ever read "Cloudy with a Chance of Meatballs"?   yes   no

How to Report on Books

Books I've Read

Topic: Snow

	yes
Does it snow where you live?	no
	yes
Have you ever built a snowman?	no

Date	Title	Author	picture ☐	Rating
		Illustrator	fiction ☐ nonfiction ☐	☆ OK ☺
Date	Title	Author	picture ☐	Rating
		Illustrator	fiction ☐ nonfiction ☐	☆ OK ☺
Date	Title	Author	picture ☐	Rating
		Illustrator	fiction ☐ nonfiction ☐	☆ OK ☺
Date	Title	Author	picture ☐	Rating
		Illustrator	fiction ☐ nonfiction ☐	☆ OK ☺
Date	Title	Author	picture ☐	Rating
		Illustrator	fiction ☐ nonfiction ☐	☆ OK ☺
Date	Title	Author	picture ☐	Rating
		Illustrator	fiction ☐ nonfiction ☐	☆ OK ☺

How to Report on Books

Topic: Birds

Books I've Read

Date	Title	Author		Rating
		Illustrator	☐ fiction ☐ nonfiction	☆ OK 😊 😞
Date	Title	Author		Rating
		Illustrator	☐ fiction ☐ nonfiction	☆ OK 😊 😞
Date	Title	Author		Rating
		Illustrator	☐ fiction ☐ nonfiction	☆ OK 😊 😞
Date	Title	Author		Rating
		Illustrator	☐ fiction ☐ nonfiction	☆ OK 😊 😞
Date	Title	Author		Rating
		Illustrator	☐ fiction ☐ nonfiction	☆ OK 😊 😞
Date	Title	Author		Rating
		Illustrator	☐ fiction ☐ nonfiction	☆ OK 😊 😞

Did you read any bird books about endangered varieties?　　yes　　no

Have you ever had a pet bird?　　yes　　no

Did you learn anything new about birds?　　yes　　no

Is a bird a good character to have in a story?　　yes　　no

Why? _____

How to Report on Books

Books I've Read

Topic: Feeling

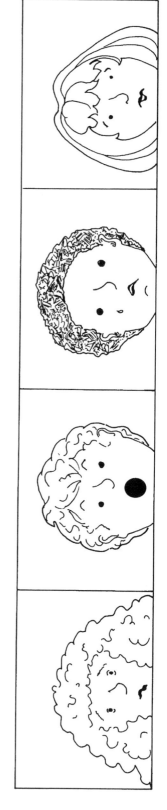

Date	Title		Rating		How did the main character feel?
	Author				
	Illustrator				
Date	Title		Rating		How did the main character feel?
	Author				
	Illustrator				
Date	Title		Rating		How did the main character feel?
	Author				
	Illustrator				
Date	Title		Rating		How did the main character feel?
	Author				
	Illustrator				
Date	Title		Rating		How did the main character feel?
	Author				
	Illustrator				
Date	Title		Rating		How did the main character feel?
	Author				
	Illustrator				

How do you feel about these books?
Were you excited about some of them?
Put a red line under your favorites.

How to Report on Books

Books I've Read

Topic: Elephants

Date	Title	Author / Illustrator	fiction / picture / nonfiction	Rating
		Author	☐ fiction ☐ picture ☐ nonfiction	☆ OK 😞
		Illustrator		
		Author	☐ fiction ☐ picture ☐ nonfiction	☆ OK 😞
		Illustrator		
		Author	☐ fiction ☐ picture ☐ nonfiction	☆ OK 😞
		Illustrator		
		Author	☐ fiction ☐ picture ☐ nonfiction	☆ OK 😞
		Illustrator		
		Author	☐ fiction ☐ picture ☐ nonfiction	☆ OK 😞
		Illustrator		
		Author	☐ fiction ☐ picture ☐ nonfiction	☆ OK 😞
		Illustrator		

My favorite elephant book is: _____

How to Report on Books

Topic: Space

Books I've Read

Date	Title	Author		Rating
		Author	☐ picture ☐ fiction ☐ nonfiction	☆ OK ☹ ☐ accurate ☐ inaccurate
		Illustrator		
		Author	☐ picture ☐ fiction ☐ nonfiction	☆ OK ☹ ☐ accurate ☐ inaccurate
		Illustrator		
		Author	☐ picture ☐ fiction ☐ nonfiction	☆ OK ☹ ☐ accurate ☐ inaccurate
		Illustrator		
		Author	☐ picture ☐ fiction ☐ nonfiction	☆ OK ☹ ☐ accurate ☐ inaccurate
		Illustrator		
		Author	☐ picture ☐ fiction ☐ nonfiction	☆ OK ☹ ☐ accurate ☐ inaccurate
		Illustrator		
		Author	☐ picture ☐ fiction ☐ nonfiction	☆ OK ☹ ☐ accurate ☐ inaccurate
		Illustrator		

Would you travel to another planet if you had the chance? **yes** **no**

How to Report on Books

Topic: Eskimos

Books I've Read

Eskimos Folktales

Title		Author
		Illustrator
Date	Main characters names:	

Title		Author
		Illustrator
Date	Main characters names:	

Title		Author
		Illustrator
Date	Main characters names:	

Books about Eskimos

Title		Author
		Illustrator
Date	Rating ☆ OK :)	When was this book written?
fact ☐ fiction ☐		

Title		Author
		Illustrator
Date	Rating ☆ OK :)	When was this book written?
fact ☐ fiction ☐		

Title		Author
		Illustrator
Date	Rating ☆ OK :)	When was this book written?
fact ☐ fiction ☐		

Tell one way life has changed for the modern Eskimo.

Books I've Read

Topic: Rabbits and Hares

cottontail

English lop

jack rabbit

Arctic hare

English spot

What are the differences between a rabbit and a hare?

Date	Title	Author		fiction	nonfiction
		Illustrator		☐ fiction	☐ nonfiction
Date	Title	Author		☐ fiction	☐ nonfiction
		Illustrator		☐ fiction	☐ nonfiction
Date	Title	Author		☐ fiction	☐ nonfiction
		Illustrator		☐ fiction	☐ nonfiction
Date	Title	Author		☐ fiction	☐ nonfiction
		Illustrator		☐ fiction	☐ nonfiction
Date	Title	Author		☐ fiction	☐ nonfiction
		Illustrator		☐ fiction	☐ nonfiction
Date	Title	Author		☐ fiction	☐ nonfiction
		Illustrator		☐ fiction	☐ nonfiction

Which fiction book here gets the highest rating?

Which nonfiction book was the best?

Topic: Fairy Tales

Books I've Read

Where do you find fairy tales in the library?

Date	Title	Author	Illustrator	Country of origin	Have you read any other versions of this same tale? yes no	Illustrated by:

What fairy tale is your favorite?

How to Report on Books

Topic: Hippos

Books I've Read

Date	Title		Rating
	Author	☐ picture	☆
		☐ fiction	OK
	Illustrator	☐ nonfiction	☹
Date	Title		Rating
	Author	☐ picture	☆
		☐ fiction	OK
	Illustrator	☐ nonfiction	☹
Date	Title		Rating
	Author	☐ picture	☆
		☐ fiction	OK
	Illustrator	☐ nonfiction	☹
Date	Title		Rating
	Author	☐ picture	☆
		☐ fiction	OK
	Illustrator	☐ nonfiction	☹
Date	Title		Rating
	Author	☐ picture	☆
		☐ fiction	OK
	Illustrator	☐ nonfiction	☹
Date	Title		Rating
	Author	☐ picture	☆
		☐ fiction	OK
	Illustrator	☐ nonfiction	☹

What does the name hippopotamus mean? _____

In what country do you find wild hippos today? _____

What do hippos eat? _____

How to Report on Books

Books I've Read

Topic: Humorous Books

Date	Title		How much did you laugh?
	Author	☐ picture	How much did you laugh?
	Illustrator	☐ fiction ☐ nonfiction	a little a lot
Date	Title		How much did you laugh?
	Author	☐ picture	
	Illustrator	☐ fiction ☐ nonfiction	a little a lot
Date	Title		How much did you laugh?
	Author	☐ picture	
	Illustrator	☐ fiction ☐ nonfiction	a little a lot
Date	Title		How much did you laugh?
	Author	☐ picture	
	Illustrator	☐ fiction ☐ nonfiction	a little a lot
Date	Title		How much did you laugh?
	Author	☐ picture	
	Illustrator	☐ fiction ☐ nonfiction	a little a lot
Date	Title		How much did you laugh?
	Author	☐ picture	
	Illustrator	☐ fiction ☐ nonfiction	a little a lot

Did you share any part of these books with a friend? yes   no
Did you read a book that was so good you might want to read it again? yes   no

How to Report on Books

Books I've Read

Topic: Friends

Date	Title		picture · fiction · nonfiction	Would you suggest this book to your friend? yes no
	Author		☐ picture ☐ fiction ☐ nonfiction	
	Illustrator			
Date	Title		☐ picture ☐ fiction ☐ nonfiction	Would you suggest this book to your friend? yes no
	Author			
	Illustrator			
Date	Title		☐ picture ☐ fiction ☐ nonfiction	Would you suggest this book to your friend? yes no
	Author			
	Illustrator			
Date	Title		☐ picture ☐ fiction ☐ nonfiction	Would you suggest this book to your friend? yes no
	Author			
	Illustrator			
Date	Title		☐ picture ☐ fiction ☐ nonfiction	Would you suggest this book to your friend? yes no
	Author			
	Illustrator			
Date	Title		☐ picture ☐ fiction ☐ nonfiction	Would you suggest this book to your friend? yes no
	Author			
	Illustrator			

Are friendship books always about people?   yes   no

Did you read about any unusal friendships?   yes   no

Why were they unusual? _____

Topic: Monsters

Books I've Read

Date	Title	Author / Illustrator	picture / fiction / nonfiction	What type of monster was in this story?
		Author ___ Illustrator ___	☐ picture ☐ fiction ☐ nonfiction	
		Author ___ Illustrator ___	☐ picture ☐ fiction ☐ nonfiction	
		Author ___ Illustrator ___	☐ picture ☐ fiction ☐ nonfiction	
		Author ___ Illustrator ___	☐ picture ☐ fiction ☐ nonfiction	
		Author ___ Illustrator ___	☐ picture ☐ fiction ☐ nonfiction	
		Author ___ Illustrator ___	☐ picture ☐ fiction ☐ nonfiction	

Do you know any monsters? ☐

How many monsters can you name in one minute?
(Write them down on the back of this paper)

Topic: Riddle Books

Books I've Read

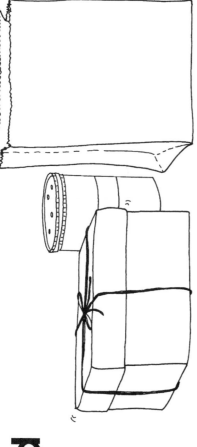

Where do you find
riddle books in the library?

_____

Date	Title	Author	Rate the riddles:
		Illustrator	good fair poor
Date	Title	Author	Rate the riddles:
		Illustrator	good fair poor
Date	Title	Author	Rate the riddles:
		Illustrator	good fair poor
Date	Title	Author	Rate the riddles:
		Illustrator	good fair poor
Date	Title	Author	Rate the riddles:
		Illustrator	good fair poor
Date	Title	Author	Rate the riddles:
		Illustrator	good fair poor

Write your favorite
riddle here.

Books I've Read

Topic: Spiders

Date	Title	Author / Illustrator	Check one.
		Author	fiction ☐
		Illustrator	nonfiction ☐
		Author	fiction ☐
		Illustrator	nonfiction ☐
		Author	fiction ☐
		Illustrator	nonfiction ☐
		Author	fiction ☐
		Illustrator	nonfiction ☐
		Author	fiction ☐
		Illustrator	nonfiction ☐
		Author	fiction ☐
		Illustrator	nonfiction ☐

Spider facts I learned.

How to Report on Books

Topic: Inventions

Books
I've Read

Date	Title	Author	☐ Fiction	Invention
		Illustrator	☐ Nonfiction	
Date	Title	Author	☐ Fiction	Invention
		Illustrator	☐ Nonfiction	
Date	Title	Author	☐ Fiction	Invention
		Illustrator	☐ Nonfiction	
Date	Title	Author	☐ Fiction	Invention
		Illustrator	☐ Nonfiction	
Date	Title	Author	☐ Fiction	Invention
		Illustrator	☐ Nonfiction	
Date	Title	Author	☐ Fiction	Invention
		Illustrator	☐ Nonfiction	

Where in the library did you find books about inventions?

Books I've Read

Topic: Monkeys

Do all monkeys have tails?   yes   no

What do monkeys like to eat? _____

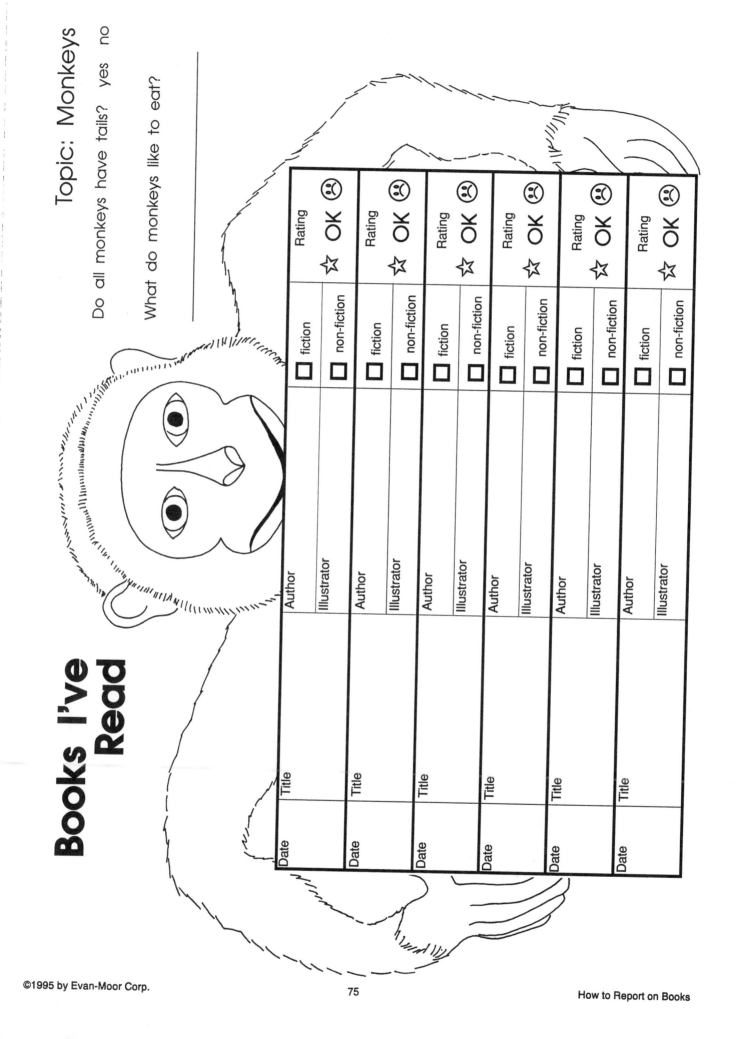

Date	Title	Author / Illustrator		Rating
Date	Title	Author	☐ fiction ☐ non-fiction	☆ OK 😞
Date	Title	Illustrator		
Date	Title	Author	☐ fiction ☐ non-fiction	☆ OK 😞
Date	Title	Illustrator		
Date	Title	Author	☐ fiction ☐ non-fiction	☆ OK 😞
Date	Title	Illustrator		
Date	Title	Author	☐ fiction ☐ non-fiction	☆ OK 😞
Date	Title	Illustrator		
Date	Title	Author	☐ fiction ☐ non-fiction	☆ OK 😞
Date	Title	Illustrator		
Date	Title	Author	☐ fiction ☐ non-fiction	☆ OK 😞
Date	Title	Illustrator		

How to Report on Books

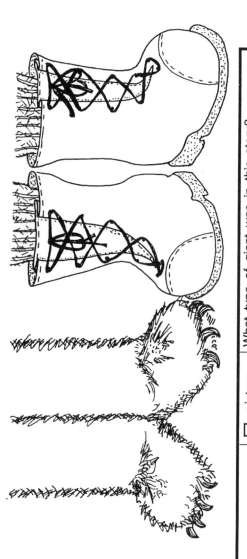

Topic: Giants

Books I've Read

Giants

Something with great size, strength or ability.

Date	Title	Author	What type of giant was in this story?
		Illustrator	☐ picture ☐ fiction ☐ nonfiction
Date	Title	Author	What type of giant was in this story?
		Illustrator	☐ picture ☐ fiction ☐ nonfiction
Date	Title	Author	What type of giant was in this story?
		Illustrator	☐ picture ☐ fiction ☐ nonfiction
Date	Title	Author	What type of giant was in this story?
		Illustrator	☐ picture ☐ fiction ☐ nonfiction
Date	Title	Author	What type of giant was in this story?
		Illustrator	☐ picture ☐ fiction ☐ nonfiction
Date	Title	Author	What type of giant was in this story?
		Illustrator	☐ picture ☐ fiction ☐ nonfiction

Do you know any giants? yes no

How many giants can you name in one minute?
(Write them down on the back of this paper)

Topic: Animals Who Live in a Shell

turtle
snail
oyster
clam
armadillo
beetle
abalone

Other:
_____
_____
_____
_____

Books I've Read

Date	Name of Animal	Title	Author / Illustrator	Circle one.	Rating
			Author / Illustrator	☐ fiction ☐ nonfiction	
			Author / Illustrator	☐ fiction ☐ nonfiction	
			Author / Illustrator	☐ fiction ☐ nonfiction	
			Author / Illustrator	☐ fiction ☐ nonfiction	
			Author / Illustrator	☐ fiction ☐ nonfiction	
			Author / Illustrator	☐ fiction ☐ nonfiction	

How to Report on Books

Bibliography

Dogs
A Bag Full of Pups by Daniel Gackenbach; Houghton Mifflin, 1981.
Daniel's Dog by Jo Ellen Bogart; Scholastic, 1990.
A Dog's Body by Joanna Cole; Morrow, 1986.
Where the Red Fern Grows by Wilson Rawls; Bantam, 1961.

Pumpkins
The Halloween Pumpkin Smasher by Judith St. George; Putnam, 1978.
Pumpkin, Pumpkin by Jeanne Titherington; Greenwillow, 1986.
The Vanishing Pumpkin by Tony Johnston; Putnam, 1978.

Bears
Big Bad Bruce by Bill Peet; Houghton Mifflin, 1977.
The Biggest Bear by Lynd Ward; Houghton Mifflin, 1952.
Blueberries for Sal by Robert McCloskey; Puffin, 1948.
Grizzly Bears by John L. Weaver; Dodd, 1982.

Grandparents
Grandma's Baseball by Gavin Curtis; Crown, 1990.
The Patchwork Quilt by Valerie Flournoy; Dutton, 1985.
The Wednesday Surprise by Eve Bunting; Clarion, 1989.
When I was Young in the Mountains by Cynthia Rylant; Dutton, 1982.

Dinosaurs
Auks, Rocks, and the Odd Dinosaur by Peggy Thomson; Thomas Y. Crowell, 1985.
Big Old Bones, A Dinosaur Tale by Carol Carrick; Clarion, 1989.
My Visit to Dinosaurs by Aliki; Harper, 1985.
New Questions and Answers About Dinosaurs by Seymour Simon; Morrow Junior Books, 1990.

Cats
A Cat's Body by Joanna Cole; Morrow, 1982.
Cat Poems by Myra Cohn Livingston; Holiday House, 1987.
A Kitten is Born by Heiderose Fisher-Nagel; Putnam, 1983.
Only the Cat Saw by Ashley Wolff; Dodd, Mead & Co., 1985.

Biography
And Then What Happened, Paul Revere? by Jean Fritz; Coward, 1982.
Carol Burnett: The Sound of Laughter by James Howe; Puffin, 1988.
Christa McAuliffe by Charlene Billings; Enslow, 1986.
Lincoln: A Photobiography by Russell Freedman; Clarion, 1987.
Pablo Picasso by Ernest Raboff; Lippincott, 1987.

Alphabet Books
A My Name is Alice by Jane Bayer; Dial, 1984.
Alphabatics by Suse MacDonald; Bradbury, 1986.
The Bird Alphabet Book by Jerry Pallotta; Charlesbridge, 1986.
I Unpacked My Grandmother's Trunk by Susan Ramsay Hoguet; Dutton, 1983.

Whales
A Pod of Gray Whales by Francois Gohier; Blake, 1988.
Humphrey, the Lost Whale by Wendy Tokuda & Richard Hall; Heian, 1987.
Sea World Book of Whales by Eve Bunting; Harcourt, 1980.
Whales by Seymour Simon; Thomas Y. Crowell, 1989.

Native Americans
Coyote and (Native American Folk Tales) by Joe Hayes; Mariposa Publishing, 1983.
The Girl Who Loved Wild Horses by Paul Goble; Aladdin, 1978.
Her Seven Brothers by Paul Goble; Bradbury Press, 1988.
Knots on a Counting Rope by Bill Martin, Jr. & John Archambault; Holt, 1987.
When Grandfather Travels into Winter by Craig Kee Strete; Greenwillow, 1979.

Bats
A Bat is Born by Randall Jarrell; Doubleday, 1978.
The Bat by Nina Leen; Holt, 1986.
Wild Babies: A Canyon Sketchbook by Irene Brady; Houghton Mifflin, 1979.
Vampire Bats by Laurence Pringle; Morrow, 1982.

Weather
Bringing the Rain to Kapiti Plain by Verna Aardema; The Dial Press, 1981.
Cloudy with a Chance of Meatballs by Judi Barrett; Atheneum, 1978.
Iva Dunnit and the Big Wind by Carol Purdy; Dial Books for Young Readers, 1985.
Storms by Seymour Simon; Morrow Junior Books, 1989.
Weather and its Work by David Lambert & Ralph Hardy; Facts on File Publications, 1984.

Snow
Snow is Falling by Franklyn M. Branley; Harper, 1986.
The Snowman by Raymond Briggs; Random House, 1986.
Katy and the Big Snow by Virginia Burton; Houghton Mifflin, 1943.
The Snow Child by Freya Littledale; Scholastic, 1978.
Winter Harvest by Jane Chelsea Aragon; Little Brown & Co., 1988.

Birds
As Dead as a Dodo by Peter Mayle; Godine, 1982.
Birds' nest by Barrie Watts; Silver Burdett, 1986.
Chicken and egg by Christine Beck & Jens Olesen; Silver Burdett, 1984.
Have You Seen Birds? by Joanne Oppenheim; Scholastic, 1986.
What is a Bird? by Ron Hirschi; Walker & Co., 1988.

Feelings
Alexander and the Terrible, Horrible, No Good, Very Bad Day by Judith Viorst; Macmillan, 1972.
Angel Child, Dragon Child by Michele Maria Surat; Scholastic, 1983.
Dinah's Mad, Bad Wishes by Barbara Jossee; Harper, 1989.
A Time for Remembering by Chuck Thurman; Simon & Schuster, 1989.
The World's Greatest Expert on Absolutely Everything is Crying by Barbra Battner; Harper, 1984.

Elephants
Elephants Big, Strong, and Wise by Pierre Pfeffer; Young Discovery Library, 1987.
The Elephant's Child by Rudyard Kipling ; Harcourt Brace Jovanovich, 1988.
All in One Piece by Jill Murphy; Putnam, 1987.
A Year in the Life of an Elephant by John Stidworthy; Silver, 1987.

Space
Charlie and the Great Glass Elevator by Roald Dahl; Bantam, 1984.
Commander Toad & the Space Pirates by Jane Yolen; Putnam, 1987.
Jupiter by Seymour Simon; Four Winds, 1985.
Space Case by Edward Marshall; Dial, 1982.
The Sun Our Nearest Star by Franklyn M. Branley; Thomas Y. Crowell, 1988.

Eskimos
An Eskimo Family by Bryan & Cherry Alexander; Lerner, 1985.
Eskimos--The Inuit of the Arctic by J. H. Smith; Rourke Corp., 1987.
I Can Read About Eskimos by Ellen Schultz; Troll, 1979.
Shadow Bear by Joan Hiatt Harlow; Doubleday, 1981.
Song of Sedna by Robert San Souci; Doubleday, 1981.

Rabbits
Bunnicula by Deborah & James Howe; Atheneum, 1979.
The Easter Bunny that Overslept by Priscilla & Otto Friedrich; Lothrop, Lee & Shepard, 1957.
Humbug Rabbit by Lorna Balian; Abingdon Press, 1974.
The Rabbit in the Fields by Jennifer Coldrey; Stevens Inc., 1987.

Fairy Tales
The Emperor's New Clothes by Nadine Bernard Westcott; Atlantic Monthly Press, 1984.
It Could Always Be Worse by Margot Zemach; Scholastic, 1976.
Jack and the Beanstalk by Beatrice Schenk de Regniers; Atheneum, 1985.
Yeh Shen by Ai-Ling Louie; Putnam, 1982.

Hippos
George and Martha, Tons of Fun by James Marshall; Houghton Mifflin, 1980.
Hippopotamus by Mary Hoffman; Raintree, 1985.
Sophie and Jack Help Out by Judy Taylor; Putnam, 1984.
There's a Hippopotamus Under My Bed by Mike Thaler; Watts, 1977.

Humorous Books
Jokes and More Jokes by Sandra Ziegler; Childrens Press, 1983.
Oh, Were They Ever Happy! by Peter Spier; Doubleday, 1978.
The Old Joke Book by Janet & Allen Ahlberg; Penguin, 1987.
Ramona the Pest by Beverly Cleary; Morrow, 1968.
Superfudge by Judy Blume; Dell, 1981.

Friends
Bridge to Terabithia by Katherine Patterson; Harper & Row, 1972.
Do Bananas Chew Gum? by Jamie Gilson; Lothrop, 1980.
Frog and Toad Together by Arnold Lobel; Harper & Row, 1971.
Nettie Joe's Friends by Patricia McKissack; Knopf, 1989.
Your Best Friend Kate by Pat Brisson; Bradbury Press, 1989.

Monsters
Clyde Monster by Robert Crowe; Dutton, 1976.
The Island of the Skog by Steven Kellogg; Dial Press, 1971.
The Judge: An Untrue Tale by Harve Zemach; Farrar, 1969.
Where the Wild Things Are by Maurice Sendak; Harper & Row, 1963.

Riddle Books
A Raft of Riddles by Giulio Maestro; Houghton Mifflin, 1983.
Remember the A La Mode! Riddles and Puns by Charles Keller; Prentice, 1983.
Sports Riddles by Joseph Rosenbloom; Harcourt Brace Jovanovich, 1984.
Tyrannosaurus Wrecks: A Book of Dinosaur Riddles by Noelle Sterne; Harper, 1979.
What Do You Call a Dumb Bunny? by Marc Brown; Random House, 1983.

Spiders
The Lady and the Spider by Faith NcNulty; Harper & Row, 1986.
The Spiders Dance by Joanne Ryder; Harper & Row, 1981.
Spider in the Sky by Anne Rose; Harper & Row, 1978.
Spiders in the Fruit Cellar by Barbara Joosse; Knopf, 1983.
Spiders by Jane Dallinger; Lerner, 1981.

Inventions
The Invention Book by Steven Caney; Workman Publishing, 1985.
The Invention of Ordinary Things by Don Wulffson; Lothrop, Lee & Shepard, 1981.
Small Inventions that Make a Big Difference by Donald Crumb; National Geographic, 1984.

Monkeys
Monkey in the Middle by Eve Bunting; Harcourt, Brace Jovanovich, 1984.
The Monkey and the Crocodile by Paul Galdone; Seabury Press, 1969.
Curious George Takes a Job by H. A. Rey; Houghton Mifflin, 1947.
Summer of the Monkeys by Wilson Rawls; Doubleday, 1977.
Monkeys and Apes by Kathryn Wentzel Lumley; Childrens Press, 1982.

Giants
The Book of Giant Stories by David L. Harrison; American Heritage Press, 1972.
Fin M'Coul: The Giant of Knockmany Hill by Tomie de Paola; Holiday, 1981.
Gulliver's Travel by Johnathan Swift; Morrow, 1984.
Jack and the Beanstalk by Lorinda Bryan Cauley; Putnam, 1983
Seven in One Blow by Freire Wright & Michael Foreman; Atheneum, 1980.

Animals Who Live in a Shell
A First Look at Sea Shells by Millicent Selsam & Joyce Hunt; Walker and Company, 1983.
A Snail's Pace by Lilo Hess; Scribners, 1974.
The Snail's Spell by Joanne Ryder; Warne, 1982.
It's Easy to Have a Snail Visit You by Caroline O'Hagan; Lothrop, Lee & Shepard, 1980.